The Kingdom Call

Gayle Garcia

TRILOGY CHRISTIAN PUBLISHERS

TUSTIN, CA

Trilogy Christian Publishers
A Wholly Owned Subsidiary of Trinity Broadcasting Network
2442 Michelle Drive
Tustin, CA 92780

Cover design by: Jeff Summers

For information about special discounts for bulk purchases, please contact Trilogy Christian Publishing.

Trilogy Disclaimer: The views and content expressed in this book are those of the author and may not necessarily reflect the views and doctrine of Trilogy Christian Publishing or the Trinity Broadcasting Network.

Manufactured in the United States of America

10 9 8 7 6 5 4 3 2 1

Library of Congress Cataloging-in-Publication Data is available.

ISBN: 978-1-63769-550-0

E-ISBN: 978-1-63769-551-7

Contents

Preface

In a world where the frightening and unexpected can be found around every corner, I have watched and been inspired by many amazing women who have shown me what real strength and character look like. I have met with women in prison whose stories are hair-raising, and that is just their childhood. I have spoken to mothers who have such dedication to their children that no illness, disability, or mental health issue can diminish their love for them but, in fact, seems to bolster it, causing it to rise up in strength.

I have been prayed for by women with healing in their hands and spoken over by those who carry the gift of prophecy. This story is about all of them. It provides proof of God's power in their lives. It provides proof of God's power in my life. I am not well educated. I am not wealthy. I show up at work day in and day out like most of you, trying to make my way in this world. The only significant thing about me is the God I have come to know. He is gracious and powerful. He is my healer and my king. He defends, protects, and provides for me. He is near. If I could shout from the mountain tops to tell the world of His great love, it would not be enough to repay Him for all He has done for me. So, I write. I do so in hopes that the words on this page will inspire you to seek His face. I write in hopes that you will feel His presence and come to know the truth, that we all have a kingdom call.

Book 1:
I Am Glorious

Lost

One never knows where life's journey will lead, as is evidenced here in the story of Glorious, the Healing Warrior. She had come from a family of Healers. Both her mother and father had been in the business of caring for those who were wounded and weak. Her growing years were spent at her parent's bakery. They were generous to those around them, giving out bread and other goodies to anyone in need. Glorious noticed that the loaves of bread called the Bread of Life gave an especially strong healing that seemed to last long after the loaf was gone.

Her parent's generosity often led them into difficulties in paying for the roof over their heads. They had debts they sometimes couldn't pay but told Glorious that the Ruler of the Kingdom that Reigns Forever promised them that their generosity would be rewarded. That someday, a young woman would enter their bakery and leave behind a blue gemstone that would be worth enough to cover all their needs for the rest of their days. Glorious loved to listen to the story and would watch expectantly for this young woman to enter their doorway and free them of the weight of their debt. Her parents also spoke of a mighty warrior called Champion who would rise up to help set all people free. They said that her strength and beauty were beyond all others and that her red hair danced like flames in the wind. Glorious yearned to meet them both.

Like her parents, Glorious knew she had the gift of healing. It was in her words and in her hands, too. As a child, her time was spent healing small woodland animals and even easing the doubts and fears of her playmates. It seemed as if her path had been laid out for her long before she had ever begun to walk it. There was only one problem with the path. As Glorious grew, she began to feel that she did not want to follow it. At first thought, she liked the idea of healing others, but then something welled up within Glorious that turned her thoughts to other things. She watched and saw how some around her strayed from their paths, talking of unimportant things as if they held value and acting in ways that brought the demon of Self-Importance to bear down upon them and steal their ability to help others. She watched them consume nectar from the Well of Deceit and engage in every wicked thing. Glorious' mouth burned with the desire to taste the nectar from the well. She longed to parade with vulgar words replacing the healing words she was given. She buried the knowledge of who she was and what she was called to do so deep within her that, one day, she simply could not see it at all and gave in to her yearning.

Making her way quietly to the Well of Deceit, Glorious tried to appear confident. The others at the well recognized at once that she was not really one of them. They knew everyone who gathered there. They could tell by the purity that surrounded Glorious that she had never been there before. The walk to the Well of Deceit had taken longer than it should have. It was just outside of the village, but Glorious' steps were hesitant, slowing her progress. Smiling nervously as she entered the group, she felt awkward and self-conscious. Some from the group began whispering amongst themselves, while others began to circle her, smiling and encouraging her to have a drink with them. Glorious could see their disease. She could see that they needed healing, but she wanted so much to be accepted that she pushed those thoughts from her mind. Besides, there were so many of them; how would she heal them all? Her healing powers were not yet mature, and she was sure she would fail. At least, that is what she told herself.

A smiling young woman with dark, dancing eyes approached Glorious. Her face was beautiful, her body slender and lithe. She reached her hands forward, offering a cup of nectar from the Well of Deceit. Eagerly, Glorious grasped the cup and drank from it. At once, she felt free of any thought of self-control. The demon of Self-Indulgence came to her first and told her to drink more, "After all," it said, "she wasn't hurting anyone." The truth was, she was hurting her parents a great deal. They had no choice but to stand back and watch her be overtaken by her desires. When they were unable to find her, they feared that she was in great danger. Glorious didn't care. No more would she worry about the well-being of those around her, or her own well-being either, but she would instead focus on feeding her wrong desires. Her mind was made up. It was at this moment that Glorious was visited by the demon of Self-Importance that had been hovering over the others who drank the nectar from the Well of Deceit.

It continued speaking to her, making her feel as if nothing mattered but what she wanted moment to moment. Glorious and the others would spend their days lying about in the grass that surrounded the Well of Deceit. Their behavior had the same pattern. All of those gathered would sleep until late in the day and, upon waking, would go first to the Well of Deceit and draw out the nectar. The vines dancing around the well had a hypnotizing effect so that even if they would have a second thought of not drinking from it, it would quickly be lost. No one gathered food, and no one had any means by which to obtain it. The nectar from the Well of Deceit became their only sustenance.

Their bodies withered and became small and weak. They grew more and more disheveled with each passing day. The people from the village looked at them from across the way with disgust and disdain. The group that stayed at the Well of Deceit spent their few waking hours talking with empty words that had no meaning. Their laughter was hollow and joyless. It carried the sound of an ugly cackle. As Glorious fed her desires, they grew larger and larger. And as time passed, they began to weigh down her arms and legs. On those days when she would go in search of food, she found she could no longer walk with surety or swiftness but trudged along slowly, dragging her desires along with her making little headway. The nectar from the Well of Deceit so clouded her thinking that on the rare occasions that she tried to remember the life she used to have, it was foggy and vague. Her thoughts were focused mostly on gaining more of what she wanted. It became an endless cycle of wanting, but even after gaining, not being satisfied. She always wanted more.

After many months of feeding the beasts called Self-Indulgence and Self-Importance, they had become so large that Glorious herself could barely be seen. She was small and futile in the shadow of the looming desires that now flung her to and fro as they sought to fulfill themselves. Glorious was in great danger of being crushed and broken by their every movement. She felt frightened and helpless. Day by day, Glorious' Regrets began to grow as well. Soon they were as large as her desires. It seemed there was no hope to be found. The crushing weight made it hard for her to speak or even breathe. She gasped for breath and cried out, "I'm dying." Just as Glorious had decided to breathe her last breath and melt into nothingness, she heard a strong, calming voice that came on a Warming Wind. It spoke with authority over Self-Indulgence, Self-Importance, and over her Regrets and said, "I am the way, the truth, and the life. Follow me." Glorious' heart leapt. The words "truth" and "life" resonated within her spirit. "Yes!" she cried out. As she did, her Regrets began to shrink. Then she heard the voice say, "Confess to me your wrong desires and behaviors, and I will forgive you and cleanse you from them." Glorious spoke in a loud voice of all the wrong desires she had held in her heart.

As she did, Self-Indulgence began to shrink just as her Regrets had done. Each time the voice spoke to Glorious, she responded with a resounding, "yes." With each response, Self-Importance, Self-Indulgence, and Regret shrunk further. This process continued for many days. As her desires shrunk, Glorious grew in strength. She began to ask the voice to restore her gift of caring for others and for it to replace her selfish desires. She wanted to leave the Well of Deceit and remembered her mother's stern warning of how placing one's own wrong desires above the needs of others could consume and destroy. She wondered why she had forgotten those words of wisdom for so long and how they were suddenly coming back to her now.

Moment by moment, Glorious felt her gifts growing and her wrong desires shrinking, until one day, her wrong desires were nothing more than faded memories. It was then that the calming voice instructed her to go to the village from where she had come, back to her mother and father, and for a time to work with them to help heal others. Glorious was worried that if she returned home, she would be turned away but did as instructed. With care, she rose from her place by the well. Her legs were still weak. As she tried to stand, she felt the Warming Wind come upon her and raise her up. With her arms outstretched for balance, she took one tentative step and then another. Slowly, she drew closer and closer to the village. She was hungry now and thought she could smell bread baking. She must be getting close!

As she entered the streets of her village, she saw her parent's bakery. She had made it! She got closer and closer until she was able to reach out for the door handle and slowly pull it open. With the tinkling of the bell that hung from the top of it, Glorious' father appeared. His face went pale, and his eyes grew large. He blinked and then stammered, "Is this a vision, or has my daughter returned?" "It's me, Papa. I've come home." Glorious' father cried out for his wife to come quickly. She had been in the upper room, doing her daily chores. Glorious heard the familiar squeak from the loose stair at the top of the staircase as her mother hurried to see what was happening. When she reached the bottom stair, her knees nearly gave out as she saw her beloved daughter standing in the bakery. She stood and stared for a moment as if she couldn't believe her eyes. Then, without warning, was upon Glorious, smothering her with kisses and hugs, talking and asking questions so quickly that Glorious could not keep up in answering them. Glorious' father came from behind the bakery counter with a loaf of fresh bread and nectar from some sweet berries and encouraged her to eat.

After the initial shock of seeing her again, her parents held her as they rejoiced over her. She had been welcomed back with open arms. Little by little, as Glorious recovered, she worked alongside her parents, using the gift of healing in her words and in her hands to help many lost and injured souls to cross over into healing. Her parents watched over her carefully, fearing she would return to her previous ways, but each time Glorious felt a thirst for wrong things, she would ask the voice that comes on the Warming Wind to come and blow away those desires. As she worked alongside her parents, healing those who were weak and broken, she met many who had also been victims of Self-Indulgence and Self-Importance, and eventually Regret. She could see the pain in their eyes as they gasped for breath. She understood it immediately and spoke truthfully and clearly to them even as she bound their wounds and gave them comfort. She was strong and firm, yet loving and kind. She told those who were injured of the Kingdom that Reigns Forever and how the voice that comes on the Warming Wind had helped heal her.

The more she used her gifts, the more knowledge she gained, the better able she was to help and to heal the injured, and with that, the happier she became. The wounded under her care seemed to sense that she had once been injured too. Finally, the day arrived when the voice that comes on the Warming Wind spoke to her and said, "Your time has come. Arise." Glorious felt a peace flood her heart. She had always known that she would be asked to return to the path that had once been set out for her. The following morning, she arose early, and with the well wishes of her parents, began her journey to the hillside where the Healing Rooms were held. As she neared, she could hear the Worshipping Warriors singing. They seemed to always be singing.

Where I Belong

Glorious followed the singing and soon came upon a shimmering orb at the top of a hill. She knew instinctively that she had reached her destination. Suddenly, Glorious became fearful and reluctant. "Would she be good enough?" she wondered. Were there others within the shimmering orb who had been lost in wrong thinking like she was but were still allowed to enter in? She continued her forward movement, all the while wondering what she would find. She watched as others tried to press into the orb. Panic welled up within her. Then she heard the voice that comes on the Warming Wind speak to her and say, "Remember, I have called you to this place." Glorious felt her fear subside. Standing next to the shimmering orb now, she reached out to touch it. In an instant, she was within the walls.

The singing that she heard from the outside was even more beautiful than she could have imagined! It sent shivers up her arms, and a smile formed effortlessly on her lips. She looked at her surroundings and found that she was standing in a curved hallway. The surface of the walls was smooth and white. To her left was one doorway, with another doorway further down to her right. She wasn't sure which way to turn, so she decided to go through the one nearest her. She turned left and entered into a room filled with the injured and the sick resting in beautiful hammocks hanging on silver threads. Her eyes grew large as she took in the view.

Healing Warriors dressed in shimmering white garments covered in beautiful gems were working, changing bandages, speaking gentle words of love, and singing songs of kindness over the injured and sick. She watched as a Healing Warrior stroked the forehead of one patient in great pain and saw that it gave immediate relief. Her heart leapt with joy. Glorious knew she had chosen the right door. She knew she was where she belonged. A Healing Warrior approached Glorious and said, "It's so nice to finally meet you." "I am Sacrifice. I have been watching you for a very long time, waiting for you to arrive. You will one day be a great Healer. The outcome of the final battle will rest partially in your healing hands. Come now. Your training will begin." Glorious began training immediately. The singing that surrounded her lifted her spirit and gave her inner peace.

Following Sacrifice day after day, she learned much more than she knew she could. There were healings of every kind. Some had bodies that had betrayed them, others gaping wounds that could only be seen by the eyes of someone like Glorious, who had the gift of healing. The hardest of all to treat were the injuries of those who had been deeply wounded by someone who should have taken care of them. Those wounds took the longest to heal.

A Day of Importance

On one particular day, after many months of training, Sacrifice came to Glorious and said, "We must
speak. Please follow me." Glorious followed her down
the hallway, passed the curved wall, and into a room
that she had never seen before. Her eyes widened as she
looked around. The room was large, with smooth, white
walls. In the center of it was an oval table surrounded
by chairs. Above the table was a glistening image of a
city filled with inhabitants bustling about their day.
This was happening in real-time as if it was a portal by
which to view the world. On the other side of the table stood a woman with such strength and beauty that
Glorious simply could not look away. Her hair was red
and danced about her as if blown by the wind, yet there
was no wind in this room at all. She wore armor covered
with gems that gleamed in the light. In awe, she spoke

hesitantly and said, "You must be Champion. I have heard stories of a mighty warrior who stands for the Kingdom that Reigns Forever. The images of you I had imagined are pale and weak compared to the beauty that radiates from within you that I see before me now." With these words, Glorious knelt. "Arise," Champion replied. "I am a servant, the same as you. The Ruler of the Kingdom that Reigns Forever has fitted us for different tasks, but we are equals in every way. I am not gifted in healing as you and Sacrifice are, and we will need your services soon. One is coming who needs to be healed. Her name is Marvelous. On her journey here, she was deeply wounded. You will take charge of her. You will see her fit to perform her task. She is a protector of the lost and wounded. She must be strong and well above all others to accomplish her assignment." Glorious nodded. Champion turned away and again focused on her work. Sacrifice motioned for Glorious to follow her, and together they left the room. Once outside the door, Sacrifice spoke, "There is one more thing I need to show you." They walked down the hallway to another door. Sacrifice motioned for Glorious to step inside. As she did, her ears, heart, and soul were filled with the same beautiful music that she heard while she was working in the Healing Room. She looked around to see sets of beautiful armor hanging on silver strands. One particular set drew her attention. "This is the most beautiful of them all," Glorious whispered. "That's because it is yours," replied Sacrifice. Glorious stepped towards it and reached out her hand. As she did, the armor was suddenly upon her! Glorious looked down at herself in amazement! She felt a surge of strength and kindness run through her. Smiling, Sacrifice said, "You are ready now."

Being so completely captivated by her own transformation, Glorious had not noticed the Worshipping Warriors surrounding the room. She looked up now and saw one of the Worshipping Warriors standing on a tower far above the rest. Knowing her question, Sacrifice said, "That is Victorious. She is the leader of the Worshippers. Her voice pierces the darkness and leaves the enemy weak. The Ruler of the Kingdom that Reigns Forever has gifted her so. She will sing, you will heal, and Marvelous, the one you have been given charge over, will protect the weak. Once she arrives, the team will be nearly complete. We will be waiting for one other. She is a scribe. Her name is Clarity."

The End

Book 2:

I Am Marvelous

I Am Marvelous

She was born on a nearly perfect day. The sun shone warmly, and the breeze blew gently over the grass while the birds chirped joyfully in the sky. Her parents, though practical people, were so deeply moved by her birth that they felt as if time itself were standing still. She was lovely and delicate with a fierce cry and fist held high in the air. She was the perfect combination of soft yet strong. Her father named her in a moment with words uttered directly from his heart. "She is marvelous," he breathed, and all of the creatures of the Kingdom that Reigns Forever joined with him in praise of her loveliness. And so it was that she was given her name. She would be called Marvelous. Her parents loved her so. They did their very best to teach her what was right and what was good and gave her every practical thing they thought she would need.

At the celebration of her tenth year, they gave her a special gift, a gilded gown. In her village, it was a right of passage. All female children at the celebration of their tenth year were given a gilded gown. But this was no ordinary gown. It was indeed quite rare. You see, the gilded gown would always be a perfect fit. As Marvelous grew, the gilded gown would grow with her. With each passing year, it would display a new, brightly colored stone. Each gown was unique to the child wearing it, with the stones representing a new skill or knowledge gained in the passing year. Once the final colored stone was in place, it would be time for Marvelous to begin her journey into a new life. The old things would be no more, and a new pathway would open up before her, and she would be on her way!

It was on the day of the celebration of Marvelous' twentieth year that her gown was finally complete, and her pathway opened up to her. Her parents, though saddened, were proud to see her journey begin. They gave her gifts to help her on her way; a satchel filled with kind words and right thinking, a leather pouch filled with water from the Well That Never Runs Dry, and finally, a hat that would cover her with wisdom and grace. Tears were shed, and goodbyes were said. Her mother's thoughts turned to all the seasons that had come and gone since the birth of her child and of how they had watched her learn and laugh and grow. She knew that it would be years before they would be reunited but held tight to the knowledge that they would one day spend eternity together in the Kingdom that Reigns Forever. She would wait expectantly for that day in hopes of seeing her marvelous girl again.

The Journey Begins

The road was smooth and wide before her, with fields of green grass and wildflowers on either side. Marvelous smiled as she took her first step forward. The sun, it seemed, was smiling too. The journey went as planned for quite some time. Marvelous felt happy and carefree. The water from the Well That Never Runs Dry had served her well, and she had only looked into the satchel of kind words and right ideas once so far. Then, without warning, in the middle of the twenty-seventh day, the sky grew dark, and the wind began to blow. It was a small storm with no rain at all that ended as quickly as it had begun. Still, it seemed an ominous warning of what might lay ahead.

As Marvelous continued on, she noticed the ground was becoming uneven and the way more difficult. The air had a chill to it, and she struggled to find her footing. She thought she heard voices on the road ahead of her, but when she strained her eyes to see, the path was clear. She stumbled over a rock in the middle of the road and nearly fell. As the evening sky darkened, Marvelous felt certain that she would be safer camping along the road. She found a large tree further up, near a bend, and decided it would be a perfect place to spend the night. Marvelous' sleep was fretful and interrupted. Her mind was filled with images of menacing faces that faded in and out.

When morning finally broke, it was wet and grey, and again, a chill filled the air. Marvelous shivered from the cold and from the memories of the images that had haunted her in the night. She reached for her pouch of water and took a long drink. It warmed her and filled her with courage. She stood to gather her belongings. As she did, she noticed that her gilded gown had gotten dirty from sleeping on the ground. She felt a tug at her heart as she tried to wipe the dirt away. It was, it appeared, there to stay. Little did she know that this was only the first of many stains that her gown would eventually have. With a sigh, she headed back towards the road to continue her journey. The road was becoming more and more treacherous. The rocks were larger now, and the incline had grown steadily steeper. The sun rarely shone, and Marvelous felt as if she were growing weaker and wearier with each step. Deep in thought as she struggled along, Marvelous felt once again that she heard voices on the road ahead. The voices would come and go yet never seemed to materialize into anything or anyone.

As she looked up, she saw a small village just at the horizon's edge. Perhaps the voices had come from there. Though it was within view, the village was still very far off. Marvelous was not sure she would reach it by nightfall. Then, suddenly, from the left, something charged her and spun her around. As it did, she heard the word, "Worthless." Stunned, she stuttered, "What did you... who...who are you?" Just then, she felt the sting of something hitting her back. "Take that, Worthless." Angered, she shouted, "I am not worthless!" Again she felt something hit her, but this time it was in the front, right in the center of her beautiful gilded gown.

As she reached to touch her dress, she realized she had been hit by filth. Someone or something was throwing filth at her. Marvelous whirled around to see a small, bent creature with the face she had seen during her night of fretful sleep. It sneered at her and growled, "Ah, I see you recognize me from your thoughts in the night. I was in fine form as I taunted you, wasn't I?" "Who are you?" Marvelous demanded. "I am the demon called Self-Loathing, and I have come to remind you of who you really are. I called you by your name, Worthless." And then, more filth hit Marvelous. As she wiped the filth from her face, she turned to see another creature. He was sneering at her, too. "Why are you doing this to me?" She demanded. In a growl, it said, "Why, it's our job, of course." Marvelous stood defiant and said, "Leave me alone," and moved towards them. They vanished and came at her from behind. "My name is Sadness," the second creature sneered, "and I will visit you often from this point on." Knowing that she was not quick enough to catch the creatures, Marvelous decided to simply move on towards her goal. With steady steps, she marched. If she could just make it to the village, she thought, then she would be okay.

The Village

Following Marvelous' every step, Self-Loathing and Sadness were never far behind. All along the way, they threw more filth at Marvelous until her beautiful gown was covered and was no longer beautiful at all. While attempting to climb one of the large boulders in her path, a portion of the hem of her gown was torn off, and she had to leave it behind, stuck on the jagged edge of the rock. As she neared the village, a third creature joined her tormentors. This one called itself Shame. It laughed at Marvelous and told her that her gilded gown was ruined and that the people in the village ahead would laugh at her and tell her she was filthy. Marvelous refused to believe it and defiantly continued on.

She felt her heart leap as she grew close enough to the village to hear the rhythmic rise and fall of voices in the streets. She approached the outskirts of town, excited at the thought of having company other than that of the three wicked creatures that were following her. She approached the main marketplace where local people were buying and selling their wares. She noticed how they glared at her and realized she looked a mess. She ducked away into a small alleyway and searched the street for a place to stay. Perhaps there was an inn. She could use one of the stones from her gilded gown as payment. Something to eat and the chance to clean up would serve her well.

A man passed by her, and as he did, she reached out to him. As she touched his arm, he turned to look at her. When he saw how dirty she was, he pulled away and said, "What do you want, you filthy creature?" Marvelous spoke softly in response and pleaded, "Please, sir, I am in need of a place to stay, food, and rest. Is there such a place in this village?" With angry tones, he replied, "No one in this village would take in one such as you. Get away from me." He turned on his heel and walked away. Marvelous was shocked and hurt by his cruel treatment. She hung her head down. Shaking with fear, Marvelous approached a woman standing nearby. The woman's reaction was much the same as the cruel man's. Marvelous tried again with a passer-by but once again received cruel treatment.

Finally, hurt and broken-hearted, Marvelous decided that perhaps she should try to find a stable to sleep in and move on in the morning. She slipped down a quiet street until she found shelter in the way of a small stable behind a tiny cottage. She bedded down in the hay, next to the animals, and tried to sleep.

Before dosing off, she looked inside her satchel of kind words and right thinking. It was nearly empty now. The hat of wisdom and grace she had been given had been torn away from her by Self-Loathing and was now lost. She took a sip from her pouch of water from the Well That Never Runs Dry, and finally feeling at peace, fell fast asleep.

The Well of Deceit

The morning dawned much too early for Marvelous. She awoke with a start as she heard footsteps approaching the stable. Standing up quickly, she attempted to gather her things and get out without being seen. She slipped out of the door and down the narrow alley, running all the way to the outer edge of town. She was out of breath and out of hope. When she finally passed the last building, she slowed her pace. Feeling weak and worthless, Marvelous thought about how her name no longer suited her. She thought about how the people of the village had treated her. As she reached for her satchel of kind words and right thinking, she realized that she must have dropped it as she fled. Now all she had left was her pouch full of water from the Well That Never Runs Dry. She was gripped by fear as she realized that if the creatures took that from her, she would be left with nothing to give her the strength to go on.

Moving along her path had become so difficult that Marvelous was no longer sure if she were even on the right road. Step by confusing step, she wandered further away. She stumbled along in tall weeds through a field that was filled with stickers and sharp rocks. They stabbed at her feet and legs and tore the fabric away from her once beautiful gown. As she wandered along aimlessly, she wondered why she had ever been born. Surely this kind of life was not worth living. No one loved her, and no one wanted her. As always, Self-Loathing, Sadness, and Shame followed closely behind, covering her with filth and ugly words as she moved along.

Feeling tired and thirsty, Marvelous began to search for a stream to get a drink. For though she still carried her pouch of water from the Well That Never Runs Dry, she no longer desired to drink from it or believed that the water would sustain her. Down a small rise, Marvelous thought she saw a well. Not fully realizing that this was a very strange place for a well to be found, she moved more quickly, with the anticipation of getting a much-needed drink. There, at the bottom of the rise, Marvelous indeed found a well. She grabbed the wooden bucket sitting on its edge and dipped it into the water. The well bubbled and splashed as if alive. The rocks surrounding it were covered with lovely green vines and bright blue flowers that were moving gently to and fro in a rhythmic dance. They seemed to be mesmerizing her. Marvelous lifted the bucket to her mouth, tipped it up, and took a sip. The water tasted like nectar, and in a moment, all of her doubts and fears faded away. She began to dance about and laugh. She felt as if she were floating on a cloud. After several hours, she began to feel sleepy and decided to lie down and rest. She slept soundly, but when she awoke, she felt weak and sick, and her thoughts were cloudy. She couldn't lift her head without feeling a terrible, stabbing pain.

At once, she remembered the nectar-like taste of the water from the well and longed to drink from it again. With each drink, she would again dance and laugh and then sleep. With each awakening, she would feel weaker than the one before, and her thoughts grew more and more cloudy. The eventual weakness from drinking at this well was so severe that Marvelous could now barely lift the bucket to her lips. She no longer laughed or danced. She could do nothing more than lay next to the well, shaking and crying. With tears rolling down her cheeks, leaving tracks in the filth thrown there by Self-Loathing, Sadness, and Shame, Marvelous cried out with her last bit of strength, "Help me!" At that moment, the sun broke through the clouds and shone down upon her. She remembered the feeling of its warmth. The three creatures that were her constant companions suddenly vanished, and a voice came to her on a Warming Wind and said, "Arise, for your time has come." Marvelous' thoughts suddenly became clear, and she remembered the pouch that she still carried that was filled with water from the Well That Never Runs Dry! "Drink no longer from the Well of Deceit," the voice said, "but drink from of the water from the Well That Never Runs Dry." Marvelous felt for the pouch, and upon finding it, drank deeply. She could feel her strength returning at once. She pulled her feet up under her and tried to stand. Her legs were weak but held. Again, she drank from the pouch. Again, her strength grew. She stood taller now and took a step. Then another.

In her eagerness to return to her pathway, she tried to move too quickly and fell. Laughing out loud, she stood again and began to run! As she looked back over her shoulder, she saw that the Well of Deceit was now a wretched black hole covered with dead branches and leaves. How had she been so fooled? How had it once looked so lovely to her? As she moved forward and further away from the Well of Deceit, she came closer and closer to her own path. She felt joy returning to her heart as the voice that came on a Warming Wind spoke to her again. "I will lead you for my name's sake. Follow me." With gentle coaxing and directing, the voice led her all the way back to her path.

To her amazement, it took little effort to navigate the steep, rocky way. Although she had sustained injuries, she was so filled with hope that she leapt from rock to rock with ease, as if being carried by the Warming Wind. In no time, Marvelous found herself at the end of her path at the bottom of a hill. The hill was covered with green grass and small white flowers. There were others on the hill, too, walking with their eyes looking up as if being drawn by something. Marvelous wondered if they had heard the voice calling them too.

As she climbed even higher, an object began to appear. It was large and round and shimmering. It was there, yet it wasn't there. Marvelous could see it, yet she could see through it as well. She watched as the others around her tried to press into the object, only to find that it was solid and could not be penetrated. Marvelous was so drawn to the beauty of its shimmering that she reached out to touch it. When she did, her hand did not hit a solid wall but seemed to pass through. Stunned, she tried it again. Again, her hand passed through. Onlookers began to gather around and watch in amazement as, over and over again, Marvelous stuck her hand through the wall. And then, suddenly, she was pulled inside in her entirety! She collapsed to her knees on a cool, white floor. As she did, a beautiful woman, clothed in gleaming armor covered with gems, came to her side and helped her stand. Marvelous was shocked to look down and see that her own tattered and filthy gown was no longer tattered and filthy, but in fact, was more brilliant and covered in more stones than it had been in its original state.

Before she could speak, the woman led her away, speaking softly and saying, "We have been waiting for you. In this place, you will be made well and whole." She led Marvelous into a large room filled with white hammocks hanging in mid-air on glistening strands of silver threads. There were women in the hammocks. They all had injuries of different kinds. The Healing Warriors were attending to their wounds and helping them heal.

The beautiful woman led Marvelous to a hammock that gently wrapped itself around her as she neared. She felt as if she were resting on a cloud. The Healing Warriors began to carefully clean and dress the wounds that she had sustained while she was lost.

Healing

After many days in the hammock being nursed back to strength by the Healing Warriors, Marvelous decided she would like to know more about her surroundings. Her wounds were nearly healed and no longer caused her pain. She let her feet slip out of the hammock and touch the floor. She stood and walked softly so as not to disturb the others. She heard singing in the distance. There seemed to always be singing. She exited the Healing Room and made her way down the hall. Soon she came upon another room.

As she peaked through the door, one of the Healing Warriors approached her and said, "This is the training room for the Princess Warriors. When you are well, this is where you will train." Marvelous turned around to find the beautiful woman who had originally helped her standing behind her. Stunned, she asked, "Princess Warriors?" "Yes, you have been called to be a Princess Warrior. Your training will begin soon." Marvelous again blinked and then stammered, "But I...don't under-stand..." Realizing she had not properly introduced her-self, Marvelous said, "I am called Marvelous." Glorious smiled and nodded, "Yes, I know. I am the Healing War-rior that helped you when you first arrived. I am Glo-rious," she replied. Smiling, she continued, "You were meant to be with us all along. You lost your way, but you made it here at last." Marvelous answered, "Yes, that is true. I finally came upon the object on the hill. I was able to press through the wall, while others were not. How could that be?" To which Glorious replied, "Only those who hear His voice may enter in. Some stumble as they eventually learn to hear His voice. Others are called but do not listen to His voice. Then there are those like you who are called, who listen, and who follow."

Marvelous eyes widened. She had heard, and she had followed. Then she asked, "There seems to always be singing here. Where does it come from?" Glorious smiled and said, "The singing comes from the Wor-shiping Warriors. Look up. They are standing on the towers above us. They sing all day and all night. They always sing. They follow the lead of Victorious. She is in charge of the Worshipping Warriors. Without their singing, the walls of this object would collapse, and we would no longer be safe from the creatures that we bat-tle." Marvelous knew at once what creatures she spoke of. She asked, "Are their names Self-Loathing, Sadness, and Shame." Glorious nodded her head and spoke, "Yes. But there are many more of them that we battle as well. We will win one day, but the fight was meant to continue for a while longer. You will be a mighty warrior soon and battle them with us." Marvelous began to feel weak again. Glorious noticed and said, "You should rest now. Your training begins tomorrow, and you will need all of your strength." Marvelous did as instructed and returned to her hammock, where she cuddled up and soon was fast asleep.

The Princess Warrior

While she slept, she dreamed. The voice she had heard when she cried out at the Well of Deceit had come to her again. She heard the words echoing, "I have not given you a spirit of fear but of power and love and of a sound mind." The voice grew louder and the words stronger as they were repeated over and over again in her mind. "I have not given you a spirit of fear but of power and love and of a sound mind." With each passing of the words, she felt her spirit rise up with strength, and her mind became clear and strong.

By morning's light, Marvelous was indeed ready, willing, and able to learn to fight. She slipped out of her hammock and walked once again down the hall to the Princess Warriors' Training Room, where the Worshipping Warriors were singing. They were singing the same words she had heard in her sleep during the night! She looked up to find one Worshipping Warrior on a tower far above the others. She must be Victorious, Marvelous thought to herself. As she stepped into the room, she noticed shimmering armor hanging in the air on silver threads. She was drawn to one set in particular. She noticed it was gilded with the same stones that were on her very own gilded gown. A Training Warrior saw her and shouted across the room, "That set of armor is for you. Try it on. You'll see that it's a perfect fit." Marvelous hesitantly reached up to touch it. It was smooth and cool.

She pulled down the Helmet of Salvation first. She tried it on and found that it was indeed a perfect fit. Next, she pulled down the Shield of Faith, then the Sword of the Word, the Breastplate of Righteousness, the Belt of Truth, and finally, the shoes of the Gospel of Peace. Like the hammock, they nearly placed themselves on her. They were light as if she wasn't wearing armor at all. They had the same shimmering beauty as the object she was now inside. She stood and watched the other Princess Warriors as they trained. She copied their moves. They came to her easily, and she began to understand that she truly was meant for this. It felt natural and, dare she say it, even fun! Her heart leapt with joy at every new truth and every new move she learned.

Day after day, Marvelous practiced. She grew stronger and quicker moment by moment, and soon she was ready to leave! On the day of her departure, she was given her pouch that was filled with the water from the Well That Never Runs Dry. She had learned to treasure it and to return to it whenever she began to feel weak. She was wearing her full armor and was more beautiful than she had ever been before. Her inner beauty shining through. Her gilded gown shone brightly beneath her armor, and she glowed with the spirit of the Kingdom that Reigns Forever. She said goodbye with haste as she was eager to be on her way. She stepped out of the safety of the shimmering orb and back into the world from where she had come. The wind felt cold and crisp, but Marvelous was ready. She stood strong.

As she expected, her old enemies, Self-Loathing, Sadness, and Shame, began to throw filth at her and tried to cover her with ugly words. Marvelous lifted her Shield of Faith, and they fell to the ground. They attacked from the left and the right, but the Sword of the Word slew them in a moment! Marvelous made her way down the hill, and as she did, she rejoiced that she would no longer be bothered by the wicked creatures. She now understood that no matter what came her way, she could overcome. There were many attacks, but Marvelous was ready for all of them. The demon called Depression tried to overtake her, but she simply moved past him with lightning speed. Gossip tried to run her down, but again, she was victorious! As her journey progressed, Marvelous began to notice things she had never seen before. To the left and to the right, on either side of her path, she saw defenseless people under attack. It reminded her of how she had once been, and her heart broke for those who had not yet learned to fight. With more courage than she had ever known, Marvelous stood between the evil creatures and the weak.

She fought for them, and every time she overcame the enemy, she directed those who had been rescued towards the hill, where her healing had taken place and her training had been made complete. She knew they would find their purpose and strength there. She asked the voice that comes on the Warming Wind, who had spoken to her, to speak to them as well. She fought, and she fought, and she fought. With every hard-won victory, Marvelous felt greater joy. With every person she helped and sent on their way, she felt encouraged, and for every day that dawned anew, she felt gratitude. She had grown into all that she was meant to be and more. Through the power of the Kingdom that Reigns Forever, she had truly become "Marvelous."

The End

Book 3:
I Am Victorious

I Am Victorious

From very early on, it was acknowledged and declared that she had been given a very special gift. Even when she was an infant, her cries had clarity and strength. All throughout her childhood, when singing for celebrations or any other gatherings, her voice stood out above the rest. It seemed to soar somehow. Stronger, louder, and more clear than all the other voices surrounding her. Her parents smiled with wonder at the gift their daughter had been given. It was as if the Mysteries themselves were made clear at the sound of her voice, and the heavens shook with eternal rewards. Her name was Victorious.

The name given to her at birth was Celeste, but very shortly into her time, it was changed by her parents to Victorious. For although her parents felt her a heavenly, celestial creature, it was clear that there was a power within this child that made Victorious a much more fitting name. In her twelfth year, a special audience was given to her by the leader of the Worshippers to stand before them and sing. News of the power of her voice had traveled far, reaching all the way to the Training Facility on the hill for the Worshipping Warriors. Upon hearing of the special request for her to come and sing, Victorious grew excited. She knew she was born for this. She felt strong and confident and happy to stand before the Leaders. She knew her voice would ring true. She knew the Mysteries would be made clear, and the veil would be lifted as her voice took flight. She just somehow knew. As the day approached, Victorious felt her voice grow. The more she sang, the more strength it gained.

Finally, the day came for her and her parents to make their way to the top of the hill. They followed pathways and trails through meadows and valleys. At times, Victorious could feel a threatening presence following them, but she would simply lift her voice and sing, and the presence would flee. After many days and nights on the road, after many stumbles over rocky, narrow paths, she found herself standing at the edge of a green meadow at the bottom of a hill. There were others on the hill, too. Victorious could see a shimmering object that was there, yet not there at all. She could see it, but she could also see through it. She stood with her parents and watched as many approached the object, slipping through the shimmering exterior and vanishing inside, while others tried to enter but would simply bounce off and be sent tumbling down the hill.

Victorious wondered why some could enter and some could not. Her parents explained that although all were invited, only those who responded to the invitation were allowed in. One could not simply enter. A reply was required. Others, her mother explained, were simply not ready yet, but would perhaps be allowed to enter at a later date, once they truly believed. Victorious was not sure she understood how she was being allowed to enter. She believed in the Kingdom that Reigns Forever and thought that must be the reason. She trusted that she had indeed been called to be a part of something much greater than herself. So up the hill, they proceeded, drawing closer and closer to the shimmering object. Victorious was quite impressed with the size of the thing. As she stood at the bottom of the hill, it looked rather small, but as she drew nearer, its true enormity was revealed. When she finally stood close enough to reach out and touch it, her mother cautioned her, "You must say goodbye to us here. Once inside, your real journey will begin. We won't see you again for a very long while." Tears filled Victorious' eyes at the thought of not seeing her parents again. Her mother, cupping her face in her hands and smiling, said, "Victorious, saying goodbye is never easy, but staying with us will not make you happy, nor will it satisfy the gift within you. You must go. You will see us again one day. Until then, we will hold you in our hearts." "But Mother," Victorious began, "I am only twelve. Surely most girls stay with their parents longer than I." Victorious' mother had prepared for this moment for many years, so her reply came swift and sure, "But not all have been given the same gift as you. Your training must begin now if your gift is to be fulfilled."

Victorious knew what her mother said was true. She felt it within, and as she did, she began to sing. As she sang, she reached out to touch the shimmering object. Her parents released her, and as they did, she found herself immediately inside. As she turned around to view her new surroundings, she saw a beautiful woman with long flowing silver hair standing in a hallway smiling at her. Victorious knew her name. She had heard it on the wind and in the air—Resonance. Victorious took a step towards her and said, "Am I to be your replacement, then?" to which Resonance nodded yes. "Shall we begin?" Victorious asked. "Follow me." Resonance spoke with a voice so lovely that it caused Victorious to shiver. "Your voice," she said, "It's more lovely than anything I have ever heard." Resonance smiled and said, "But what is needed now is strength. My voice has served the Kingdom that Reigns Forever very well. Its impact has been felt far and wide, but we are coming into a new era. The battles will increase in intensity and frequency. We have reached a time when more power is needed. That is you, Victorious. Your voice is needed for such a time as this." Her words filled Victorious with understanding, and she knew she was ready, willing, and able to fulfill her destiny.

For Such a Time as This

Following along behind Resonance, Victorious marveled at the beauty of the white floors and walls of the Training Facility. The hallway bent to the right as they walked past doors on either side. Victorious saw a room full of strong young women in armor engaging one another in sparring matches with swords and shields drawn. Another doorway led into a room full of silver hammocks hanging in the air on silver strands. There were women sleeping in some of the hammocks. It looked like a room to care for the hurting.

When Victorious had first entered the Training Facility, she heard singing. Although she had never heard the song before, the melody came easily to her, and she began to hum along. She soon began to pick up on the words as well. "He has not given me a spirit of fear but of power and love and of a sound mind. He has not given me a spirit of fear but of power and love and of a sound mind." Then, with a burst of energy, Victorious sang out, "And there is no more fear only power, no more fear only love, no more fear only power and a made-up mind coming from above." Resonance smiled as she listened to Victorious sing. This young one did indeed have a mighty gift. She would not need to sing before the Leaders to affirm her position. Her powerful voice had spoken for her as it created a vibration that resounded within the shimmering orb laying claim to the truth that she would be the next to lead the Worshipping Warriors.

Shortly, Resonance stopped and pointed towards an open door. "This is where you will be staying. You will share my quarters with me." Victorious' eyes widened, and she asked, "With you? Are you sure?" Resonance smiled and said, "My time here is nearly finished. There is no reason to let this beautiful room sit empty if I am not here. It is appointed for the Leader of the Worshipping Warriors. That is you, Victorious. You have only a short time for training, and then you will take over my position. In the Training Facility, time travels much faster than it does on the outside. You'll see. It will soon be your time to lead."

Just then, Victorious thought she heard a voice. It came to her on a Warming Wind. When she turned to see who had spoken to her, no one was there. "I thought

I just heard someone speaking to me," she said. "That was the voice that comes on the Warming Wind. It is a voice you must learn to hear loud and clear and to obey." Victorious nervously said, "It sounded like a faint whisper...how...how will I ever learn to hear it loud and clear?" Resonance placed her hand gently on Victorious' shoulder and said, "I will teach you, young one. The same way it was taught to me."

Together, they entered the room that they would share. Victorious gasped at the beauty of it. Everywhere she looked, it glistened and shimmered. There were two hammocks hanging by silver threads—one for Resonance and a smaller one for Victorious. There was a round orb on a silver table in the center of the room. Victorious wondered what it was for but didn't ask. She knew that she would learn all she needed to know as time went on. Resonance motioned towards a wall of drawers and said, "All of your belongings will be stored here. There will be books and songs and musical instruments to use for your training as well as silver gowns for you to wear." Victorious approached the wall of drawers and slowly opened one.

When she looked inside, it was empty. She turned to Resonance to ask why the drawer was empty, but before she could speak, Resonance said, "They will fill up as needed. Nothing will come before its time." On the wall next to the drawer was a mirror. When Victorious looked into it, she noticed that a few strands of her hair had turned silver. "Why is my hair silver?" she asked. Again, Resonance smiled and said, "When you are ready to take my place, your hair will be completely silver, like mine. Your transformation has already begun. You are a quick learner, Victorious, and you have indeed been called for such a time as this."

Training Day

For several weeks, Victorious was allowed to wander the halls of the Training Facility. She sang as she explored, learning every song that the Worshipping Warriors sang. She found that the facility was as round on the inside as it appeared to be on the outside. The hallway traveled in one giant circle past door after door of Healing Rooms for the Caring Warriors and Sparring Centers for the Protective Warriors. There was some type of activity going on at all hours of the day and night. And always, there was singing.

On the final day of her second week, Resonance spoke to Victorious and said, "It is time, young one. We must begin your training." Victorious heart leapt with joy and excitement! She was more than ready for this! "Tomorrow, at first light, you must be up and ready." That night, Victorious tried to sleep, but the excitement of the coming day was too much for her, and she tossed and turned in her silver hammock. With the first light, she jumped out of bed and got dressed. Hoping she would be the first one awake, she was disappointed to see that Resonance was already up and sitting at the table with the orb in the center of it. "Come join me," she said. With that, Victorious walked over to the table and pulled out a chair that had not been there before, and sat down.

Resonance then explained, "This orb is a training window. It will allow you to see both song and verse, as well as images of the terrible creatures we are fighting against. You must learn to recognize them in order to beat them. You may be frightened and upset by some of the images, but you will not be harmed. This is simply a window by which to view them. It is called the Eye of the Spirit of Truth. It is a gift from the Kingdom that Reigns Forever." As Victorious looked into the orb, she could not see anything. There was movement and blurry images, but none of them were clear or in focus. "I can't see them," she stated. "Not yet," Resonance replied, "but soon, very soon, you will." As she spoke, Victorious thought she saw an image in the orb. It was fleeting and only lasted for a moment, but Victorious was sure she had seen it! It looked like a crying child. Resonance noticed the expression on Victorious face and said, "Yes, it was the face of a crying child. She has been stricken with disease and is in pain. That is why she cries. As I said, some of the images you see will frighten and upset you, but you must learn to sing through them, for these are the things you have been called to defeat." Victorious' eyes widened and filled with tears. She suddenly felt very young and weak. This journey would be more difficult than she had imagined.

So that was it. The moment her training had begun. Day after day, she looked at the orb and was shown scenes of terror inflicted on people by the terrible creatures called Disease, Jealousy, and Lying. There were many more as well. There was Bondage and Fear, all needing to be conquered. Some days, Victorious would crumble into tears and not be able to continue on. It was at these times that Resonance would tell her to "fight on." "The more terrible the vision, the more powerful the worship must be to overcome it. Press on, sing louder, stand tall. You can win, Victorious, you can win!" Victorious would muster up all the strength she could gather, and when that wasn't enough, she would call out to the voice that comes on a Warming Wind, and her strength would increase! She would see words and songs from the orb fill the room that talked of love and grace and mercy. Some of the words on display came from Victorious herself and were sent spinning in the atmosphere as a way to overcome. Other times, the words came from the Spirit of Truth and were sung over Victorious as if they were a blanket to cover her in times of great struggle.

Silver and Gold

Month after month, it continued this way. Resonance would encourage, and Victorious would stand strong and sing! And then it happened. It came so very unexpectedly that Victorious was shocked when one morning she awoke to find that all of her hair had turned silver. She jumped out of bed and ran to the mirror to see! Her hair shimmered and danced with light. Her dress had transformed as well, and she found that the simple silver gown she had worn to bed had become a beautiful gilded gown covered with glittering gold! She looked older too. No longer a child at all.

As Victorious looked at herself, she twirled across the room with delight! Resonance watched from her hammock with a gentle smile on her face and tears in her eyes. The day had come. This brave, gifted young girl was ready. She had become as precious as silver and gold. Resonance could now go and spend forever worshipping in the Kingdom that Reigns Forever. Her mission had been fulfilled, her journey now complete.

Sensing the change in the atmosphere, Victorious turned to Resonance. Seeing the tears in her eyes, she too began to cry and said, "Not another goodbye." As she spoke, Resonance began to sparkle. As she sparkled, her image grew fainter and fainter. Victorious went to her and wrapped her arms around her, and held her tight. Resonance hugged her back and then spoke, "You must let me go now. My time has come to an end. Go and take your place on the pedestal in the Worship Room. It belongs to you now." Victorious slowly drew back from Resonance. She nodded that she understood. She had seen the Worship Room many times while exploring the Training Facility. She had seen Resonance standing on the pedestal, leading the other worshippers, and knew that she would be taking her place one day. She just didn't realize that today would be that day. "They're waiting for you, Victorious. You must go now. They're waiting for you..." With those last words, Resonance was gone. Victorious hung her head low and wiped the tears from her eyes. Then suddenly, she felt strength come into her. She lifted her head and vowed, "I will worship day and night for the sake of the Kingdom that Reigns Forever. I will fulfill my destiny. I will defeat Disease, Jealousy, and Lying, and all of the other terrible creatures with the power of worship! I will be, and *I am* Victorious!

The End

Book 4:
Call Me Clarity

The Curse

Not everyone who is called to the Kingdom that Reigns Forever is born under a blessing. Some are called out from under a curse. Clarity is one of these. There was, at some earlier time, a terrible deed done by one of her family members that covered them with a terrible curse for many generations. The curse grew more destructive with the passing of time. By the time Clarity was born, the curse had grown to ten times its original strength. In an attempt to spare her from the curse, Clarity's mother and father left her. They were hoping that by moving far away from their daughter, they would save her from the grief and poverty they had known. They even gave her the name "Clarity" in an attempt to destroy the curse of the cloudy visions of the future that the family had known for so long. You see, her family had originally been given the gift of visions and dreams of the future. When the terrible deed was committed, it blocked the visions, and without them, the family slowly began to perish. Sadly, her parent's efforts to spare their daughter only caused the curse to grow stronger. Living without parents and being abandoned only made the way more difficult for Clarity.

With no one to care for her, she was assigned to the care of the Nothing Clan. They had no faces with which to smile and no arms with which to love. They were given mechanical attachments that allowed them to do only simple chores that would enable them to provide for the children's basic needs, such as food, clothing, and limited education. As soon as Clarity could read and write, she was given over to the care of the Work House, a cold, dark place where parentless children were sent to work their way through their entire life. The Work House hours were long and hard. Some children had to shovel enormous piles of rock and debris to make way for new roads. Others were sent to clean and scrub the homes of prominent village officials. They were only allowed one day of rest each week with no eventual end in sight. This would be their fate for all of their days.

Clarity had it some better. Her job was to write down lessons for the children of the prominent village officials who were allowed to attend school in the Building of Learning. Although there were days when Clarity longed to go outside and run and play, her days at the desk in the Work House were not as bad as the long hours of hard, physical work suffered by other children.

The Work House Writing Room was filled with row after row of metal desks and chairs all filled with children like Clarity. Their work began when they rose each day and ended when the sun went down at night. The Writing Room leaders found that too many hours at the desk worked against them in the form of mistakes caused by tired eyes. Many of the children wore thick heavy glasses, their eyes damaged by overwork. Even though the days were long, Clarity found she loved words, so there was at least some small amount of joy to be found. She even tried to study the lessons she was copying in an effort to advance her own learning. It slowed her writing down a bit but was well worth the effort.

Through studying the lessons, she had learned of the Kingdom that Reigns Forever and of a voice that comes on a Warming Wind. It was told as a fable, a fairy tale, yet it seemed very real to Clarity. She longed to hear the voice that comes on a Warming Wind and wondered if she could somehow change her destiny by believing in the Kingdom that Reigns Forever. There were other children in the Writing Room who also wished to become part of the Kingdom that Reigns Forever. Without any breaks in their schedule, the children rarely had the chance to talk of such things, but on occasion, when the Writing Room leaders were distracted by outside events, the children would huddle together in a corner and whisper of the freedom that could come to them if they could only find some way to become part of the Kingdom that Reigns Forever.

Write It Down

On one particular day, Clarity felt there had been a shift in the atmosphere in the Writing Room. She found herself smiling often and had a sense of a Warming Wind blowing across her shoulders and lifting her hair ever so slightly. Was this the Warming Wind that she had heard of? Was the Kingdom that Reigns Forever reaching out to her in some mysterious way? One of the other children in the Writing Room yelled out, "Clarity! Clarity, your hair! It's moving!" No one ever yelled across the room in the Work House out of fear of the leaders.

Suddenly, all writing stopped. The room grew silent, and the children froze in anticipation of the beating that would surely come for breaking one of the Work House rules. As the children waited, they slowly began to see that none of the Writing Room leaders had seemed to hear the shout. They were still going about their business as if nothing had happened. Slowly, Clarity stood up from her chair. Her hair was now being blown across her face by a powerful wind. The children nearest to her could feel it too. It was filling the entire room, starting with Clarity!

Just then, she heard a voice say, "Write it down on tablets, make it clear. Your gift is clarity of thought. Your parents chose your name well. The curse has been lifted. Arise, Clarity, for your time has come." Clarity felt chills run across her arms and her heart began to beat rapidly. Before she knew what was happening, she felt laughter rising up within her and forming on her lips. The rest of the children began to laugh too! Though they had not seemed to have heard the voice, they were all feeling the Warming Wind. Suddenly, Clarity saw words forming on the pages that lay on the desk in front of her. As the words appeared, they grew larger. Once they became too large for the page to contain, they leapt from the page and filled the room. They swirled and danced in the air. They spelled out "hope," "joy," "peace," "freedom," and "love"! As the other children read the words in the air, their minds were filled with those very things! Then the words spelled out, "Dwell upon what is good and pure and true." The words had power and gave the children something they had never had before. Hope. The children now, for the first time ever, had hope! As the Warming Wind began to die down, Clarity stood still. She was filled with a new sense of understanding. She knew she must leave the Work House. She knew if she did, she would be protected and safe. She knew there was a road that she would travel that would lead her to a shimmering object on a hillside. She knew because she saw a vision, a view of things to come. The great visions originally given to her family were now coming upon Clarity! She sat back down at her desk and began to write.

Every word she wrote would grow too large for the page and, twirling and swirling about, would be carried on the Warming Wind to fill the room. "I have plans for you!" One set said. "I have loved you always," said another. Still, another said, "I will set you free." Clarity understood that the words were coming from the Ruler of the Kingdom that Reigns Forever. She could see it clearly. She was given a vision of the children being set free by a group of powerful warriors. She found her own face among them. She could see the children cheering in the streets, free from the Work House.

She continued to write, telling of her visions. Again, the words leapt from the page and filled the room. As they did, the children cheered! For so many years, the visions that her family had been given as a gift had gone silent.

Now, as if by some miracle, they were flooding Clarity's mind. She turned to the other children and said, "I have to go now, but I promise I will come back for you. I will bring others with me, and they will help to set you free." The children looked at each other. They knew that she was telling the truth, as the Warming Wind had begun to blow across them, lifting their spirits and filling them with laughter. They looked back at Clarity. The child who had first seen Clarity's hair move and had shouted across the room was the first to speak, "When?" She asked, "When will you come back for us?" Clarity waited for a vision to come to her, and when it did, she said, "It will be very soon. I don't know the exact day, but the Ruler of the Kingdom that Reigns Forever has a plan to set you all free. I will be back with others who will help me. There will be a mighty battle which we will win, and when it is accomplished, you will be free."

Pointing to the child who had spoken, she said, "I have seen a vision of you speaking to many and teaching them of the Kingdom that Reigns Forever. That is your gift. To proclaim the love, healing, and freedom that it brings. Proclaim it now and continue until I return. The leaders of the Work House will not stop you. You will be covered by silence even as you speak." The child spoke, "I hear your words and know that they are true. I will speak of the Kingdom that Reigns Forever until you return with the others to set us free." "There are warriors that are coming to fight back against the creatures that hold us captive. Even they will be set free. They were once children, as we are. I have seen this in a vision too." Clarity's mind was filled with vision after vision of the things to come. So many that she could barely keep them all straight.

Her first instinct was to sit back down at her desk and write them all down as they came to her, yet she knew that she must leave, that it was time for her to go. Clarity nodded to the children and turned towards the door that led to the outside world.

She was nervous as she had never been in the outside world as a free person, and she was not yet grown, only being in her sixteenth year. Her hair was stringy, and her feet were bare. Her dress was nothing more than a simple shift that was tattered and worn. The site of her was unimpressive, to say the least. As she approached the door, the ragged dress that she had worn for so many years began to transform. A mist formed around her feet and rose upward, and with it, a gown appeared and began to shimmer and sparkle. Step by step, beautiful gemstones began to shine. The Warming Wind spoke to her heart and said, "With every lesson; the patience to sit at your desk and type, the kindness you displayed in the face of cruelty from the Work House leaders, the truth you have learned about the Kingdom that Reigns Forever, you have earned your gown." For a moment, Clarity paused. She wanted to take in this moment and remember it always. By the time she was ready to exit the Writing Room, she was clothed in a beautiful gilded gown! Her eyes sparkled with delight and wonder as she looked down at her lovely dress. Her hair was smooth and soft around her face, and her feet were now covered by delicate slippers. She looked back at the children in the Writing Room one last time. They were standing transfixed by Clarity's beauty. She had been transformed from the inside out. Clarity smiled at them, waived one last time, pushed open the door, and entered the outside world.

Along the Way

Once outside, Clarity's eyes were dazzled by the loveliness she saw there. It had been so long since she had seen the outside world that she had forgotten its beauty. There were green trees and red flowers. There were rolling hills just beyond the village streets covered with tall, waving grass. The sounds were lovely as well. The sound of voices rang from the shops filled with people purchasing their wares. It had been so quiet and dark in the Work House that Clarity stopped for a moment to take in all the glory of the world that now surrounded her.

As she stood, she took a deep breath and felt certain that she recognized the scent of bread baking! She opened her eyes quickly and began to look around to see where it had come from. She took a step forward. Then another and another, feeling sure she had found the source of the scent. She walked down an alley past a large building.

When she came to the end of it, she turned to the left to see that she was standing at the entrance to a bakery! Her mouth was watering now as she entered. The baker looked up and smiled at her and said, "What can I get for you today?" Clarity replied, "I have no coins to offer as payment for bread, sir." To which the baker replied, "How about one of the gemstones from your dress? My wife would love the brilliant blue one." Clarity moved forward quickly, pulling the blue gemstone from her dress. "Sir," she asked, "I am heading out on a long journey. Would you have a satchel I could carry the bread in?" The baker smiled and said, "I can do better than that!" He disappeared through a door behind him and came back with a large woven purse with two leather handles. "Here," he said as he handed it to Clarity, "this should work fine. How much bread would you like? I'm sure that brilliant blue gemstone is worth one of everything that you see! Take what you will." Clarity smiled with delight! She chose a full loaf of bread, a scrumptious sweet cake, and four biscuits with cheese inside of them. She asked the baker if she could take one of the corked bottles filled with nectar made from wild berries, and he agreed. Clarity filled the large woven purse with her purchases, smiled, thanked the baker, and headed out the door. "Take care of yourself, Clarity," the baker said, smiling. Stunned, Clarity was unable to speak. How did he know her name? As if he knew what she was thinking, the baker spoke again, "I am part of the Kingdom that Reigns Forever," he said smiling. "I have been told of a child who would come from the Work House and ask for bread. I was told to ask for the blue gemstone from her gown as payment. The stone will provide enough for me to pay off my debt and be free of the burden of the Work House overseer. A debt I have long owed and have dreamed of being free of. Your provision for me is satisfied, as is mine for you. You have chosen well. The loaf you have chosen is the Bread of Life. The recipe came to me on the voice of the Warming Wind. Go now, quickly. There is much to be done." Clarity could only nod. Grabbing tightly to the handles of her new purse, she turned, stumbling slightly, and made her way out of the bakery.

She walked only a few yards when the smell of the food she was carrying made her mouth water so badly that she simply could not wait any longer to take a bite. She stepped out of the main thoroughfare of the street, into a small alleyway, opened her bag, and pulled out one of the biscuits filled with cheese. She ate it quickly, needing a drink of the berry nectar to wash it down. She then took out the sweet cake and tore a piece from it. She stuffed it in her mouth without manners and then stood still, with eyes closed as its wonderful sweetness filled her mouth! She chewed slowly, not wanting to rush this moment. Never in her entire life had she tasted sweet cake. Now that she had, she understood all she had missed out on while at the Work House and decided that she would enjoy every bit of everything from now on that she encountered along the way.

Finally ready to head out on the open road, Clarity placed the remainder of the sweet cake back into her large woven purse and started out. She had a vision of the shimmering object on a hill and knew which direction to head. There was a wide, open pathway leading out of town. There was grass and flowers on either side. The road was smooth and easy to travel. Clarity had no trouble walking and making good progress. She moved along happily until the sun began to set. She knew that she should rest but decided to walk just a little further. She was simply too excited to stop any sooner.

When it grew too dark for her to see the road in front of her, she decided she would lie down and rest for the night. She found a large rock on the roadside with an overhang that would shelter her. Clarity lay down in the soft grass beneath it, placed her large woven purse under her head as a pillow, and was soon sound asleep.

Daylight broke like a glorious symphony. The birds were singing, and the breeze was rustling gently in the trees. Clarity was hungry and immediately reached inside her purse for something to eat. She grabbed the loaf of bread and tore off a large piece. As she ate, she felt her strength rise up within her. This bread, the one the baker had called the "Bread of Life," seemed to fill more than just her empty stomach. It sent a calm through her entire being. She also pulled out the bottle of berry nectar. She switched back and forth between the bread and the drink until she felt satisfied and full. She immediately knew that her wisdom and gifting had grown with every bite she had taken of the Bread of Life.

She lay quietly back down in the grass for a moment, and as she did, a vision came to her. She saw creatures, evil and dirty, following her, attempting to distract her from the right path that would get her to her desired destination. She felt anger rise up within her as she vowed that nothing would stop her from reaching her goal. Just then, the Warming Wind blew across her face. As it did, her anger was subdued, and she felt the sure knowledge that she would make it to her destination by relying upon help from the Ruler of the Kingdom that Reigns Forever. She began to see that the evil, dirty creatures had no real power other than to distract and annoy, that all of the real power comes from the Warming Wind and from the Ruler of the Kingdom that Reigns Forever and with that new knowledge, Clarity stood, made her way back to her path, and continued on her way.

Distraction and Delay

Humming along cheerfully, Clarity felt as if her feet were barely touching the ground as she walked. She had always had a strong countenance and was finding that she felt more confident and fearless than ever before. Just as those thoughts went through her mind, the words leapt into the air. "Strength" and "confidence" stood in the air before her with the clear blue sky as their backdrop. Clarity was surprised. When she was in the Work House, she had to write the words on paper for them to appear, but now, they appeared from her thoughts into the sky before her! How did this happen?

She felt the Warming Wind blow across her face, and she knew. It whispered, "Now you see your gift. It will be used to set my children free. Tell them of the visions and dreams I give you. Fill the skies with my good words."

Clarity stood in awe. Surely this gift she had been given was the most wonderful of all!

In an instant, a cold blast came. It pushed at the words that stood in the sky and moved them out of view. She covered her face to protect it from the icy air. Then she reached out with her hand as if to try and catch the words before they were blown away. As she did, she felt a stinging in her fingertips and heard a deep, frightening voice that said, "Did you think you wrote words in the sky? That was nothing more than your overactive mind trying to convince you of something that wasn't real." Clarity was startled by the voice and stammered to say, "I d...d...did write them in the sky." The voice replied, "Did you? Or is it, as I said, that they were nothing more than an illusion?" Clarity looked to the sky, but the words were gone. Had she imagined it after all?

Now the voice was silent. She looked around but did not see any source from which the voice might have come. What was happening, she wondered? She began to worry. Had she left the security of the Work House for a life of danger in the outside world? Was the vision of the sphere real? Which direction should she go now? The pathway she had seen in her vision was before her but somehow looked foggy and unclear. Clarity sat down on the side of the road. "Maybe I should wait here for a little while and collect my thoughts." As she sat, morning turned to afternoon and afternoon to evening. Still, she waited.

As night fell, Clarity again placed her purse under her head as a pillow and tried to go to sleep. Sleep would not come this night. She tossed and turned. She replayed the events of the day over and over again in her head, trying to decide what was real and what was not. At sunrise, Clarity was troubled and tired. She stood slowly, forgetting to eat from the Bread of Life. She lifted her woven purse to her shoulder and looked to the road before her. There was a fork in it that had not been there yesterday, or was it, and she simply had not noticed?

Unclear about anything, she headed in the direction of what appeared to be the pathway she had seen in her vision. Her steps were slow and unsteady. Her head hurt, and she felt foggy and confused. As it had done the day before, a blast of cold air hit Clarity. She shivered as the voice spoke, "What are you doing? Why are you taking this journey? It is nothing more than a waste of time and energy. Go back to the Work House. You were safe and warm there." With tears beginning to fall, Clarity shouted in desperation, "Who are you? What do you want?" The voice fell silent again. Now it was the Warming Wind that gently blew across Clarity's face, drying her tears and lifting her hair and her spirit, and saying, "Its name is Doubt. It plagues the best of my children. Even the strong and confident like you,

Clarity. You will need to learn to ignore that voice and listen only to me." Clarity remembered the vision she had seen of evil creatures following her, and she knew that what the Warming Wind said was true.

Lifting her head, Clarity spoke aloud and said, "I am strong and confident! The Warming Wind and the Ruler of the Kingdom that Reigns Forever are with me, and I am safe!" The Warming Wind replied, "Stop and eat of the Bread of Life. You will encounter delays on the road ahead and will need the strength to continue on in spite of them." Clarity did as she was told, having learned a valuable lesson about which voice to follow. After eating, she began her journey again. The road for her now was clearly marked, and the way was easy to find.

Into the Fold

Having been given the knowledge to make her way past the distractions, Clarity made good progress on her journey. It wasn't long before she found herself at the bottom of a hill upon which she found the shimmering orb. She could hear singing. It was lovely and powerful! Clarity watched as people approached the orb. It was strange how some would approach it and be drawn immediately inside, while others would bounce off, unable to enter in. "Will I be able to enter?" She wondered to herself.

As she walked up the hill, her excitement grew. The closer she came to the orb, the louder the singing became. She could hear the words clearly now, "He has not given you a spirit of fear but of power and love and of a sound mind. He has not given you a spirit of fear but of power and love and of a sound mind." Over and over again, they would sing. It strengthened Clarity somehow, and her determination to reach the top of the hill and the orb was doubled. Finally, she arrived.

She stood next to the orb, close enough to touch it. Oh, how she wished she had a writing tool and tablets with her. She wanted to record this moment for all to read. She focused on each detail. On the people around her, those trying to get in, and those being drawn in immediately. She noticed a marked difference in the two groups. Those being drawn in were singing the worship songs and carried a light in their eyes that shone brightly. Others were held captive by evil, dirty creatures. Some held onto the creatures rather than being held by them. Clarity was not aware that what she was seeing was invisible to most. She was being given a vision. She knew she had not let the evil creatures attach themselves to her. She knew she was free and believed in the Kingdom that Reigns Forever. She felt compassion for those who were still being deceived. She decided to go to them and tell them what was holding them back.

As she approached one of them, the evil, dirty creatures hissed and spit at Clarity. She knew better than to be afraid. She pushed them aside and tried to speak. The creatures began to circle around her. She reached out to touch one of the people who was being deceived. When she did, one of the evil creatures touched them at the same time and burned their flesh. The person who had been touched turned quickly to face Clarity and, with angry words, began to attack her. Clarity was confused, not knowing what exactly was happening.

Just then, as if by magic, the Warming Wind came upon her. It spoke to Clarity alone and said, "Clarity, you are a scribe. You must write your visions down for all to read. Your spoken words fall on deaf ears. Enter now into the fold and learn how to work in your gifting to help those who have been deceived. Once you have completed that task, your spoken words will begin to have meaning. Time is of the essence. Move now!" Clarity, although regretting that she wasn't able to help anyone, did as she was told. She placed her hand inside the orb and was immediately pulled inside it.

The air inside was cool and clear. The floors and walls were white and smooth. There was a curved passageway in front of her. She began to walk down it. She looked to the left to find a doorway that led to a room full of women in shimmering gowns healing and nursing the injured back to health. To the right was a room filled with women in beautiful armor training to fight. There were also women singing songs of worship to the Ruler of the Kingdom that Reigns forever.

At the very end of the passageway was a room filled with scribes. The atmosphere above them was filled with words! Clarity felt her heart leap! "I have found it," she whispered to herself. As she surveyed the room, she noticed a large, empty desk. She was immediately drawn to it. Slowly, she entered the room and made her way towards it. The desk was lovely and shimmering, the same as everything else within the orb. It was much larger than the other desks in the room. Clarity wondered why. As if hearing her thoughts, a scholarly-looking, older woman approached her and said, "Welcome, Clarity. We've been waiting for you," and motioned towards the large desk. Clarity looked from the woman and towards the desk. She took a hesitant step forward. When she did, the atmosphere was filled with the words, "Approach quickly!" and "Your time has come!" Clarity looked around to see that all eyes were on her. There were great smiles on the faces of the other scribes in the room. They seemed to be cheering Clarity on with silent approval.

When Clarity finally reached the large, shimmering desk, her eyes widened as she saw her name written upon it. This was *her* desk! It was at the head of the room and was larger than all the others! She turned to ask the scholarly woman what this meant, and again, as if reading her mind, she said, "You have been chosen as the head scribe. Your skills learned during the long hours at the Work House are far above anyone else's. What was meant for harm will now be used for good. There is a battle coming soon. It will be the battle to end all battles. You will be the Chief Scribe. Take your seat, Clarity, so that your training may begin."

As Clarity sat, she felt visions and dreams fall upon her. Before she could lift her hand, a writing tool and a tablet appeared. Like water flowing over a waterfall, Clarity began to write. As she did, her words again leapt from the page. A collective gasp came up from the scribes around her. Never had they seen such skill and precision.

Clarity continued to write until the room was so full of words that they began to be pushed out the door into the passageway. It was then that the scholarly woman approached her and, placing a hand gently on her shoulder, said, "Slow down, Clarity. It will all come out in good time and at the proper time. You must allow the Ruler of the Kingdom that Reigns Forever to tell you when to write and when to be still. He will do this through the Warming Wind that will blow across you and speak to you. It is time to begin." With that, she moved to the front of the room and began to teach.

Life Lesson

Clarity found that her skills were much more advanced than the skills of those surrounding her. Lesson upon lesson, she was able to accomplish more than all the other scribes combined. She began to notice something else as well. When she entered the shimmering orb, she was a mere child, but as each day passed, she grew older and more mature. It was as if time had been accelerated.

When Clarity asked her instructor about the rapid growth that she was experiencing, she gently explained that the years in the Work House had slowed her growth. She was now moving towards what her true age was. Within the Kingdom that Reigns Forever, healing comes in many forms. For Clarity, it was found in becoming mature. As Clarity stood wide-eyed listening to her teacher, another question came to mind. She shifted her weight on her feet, nervous to ask. The words finally began to spill out of her, and she said, "And what about...do you know anything about...my parents?" With the kindest smile Clarity had ever seen, she answered her with a gentle voice and said, "We have been waiting for your healing to be full enough for you to ask. Your parents are here, Clarity. They were set free from the curse that covered your family on the same day that you began your journey. They are here, wishing and waiting to see you. Follow me, dear child. You will be reunited now."

Clarity's heart leapt within her chest. She had dreamed of this day. Now, looking back, perhaps that dream was a vision of her future all along. Either way, Clarity was shaking with nervous joy as her teacher led her down the hallway to a room she had never seen before. "This is the Room of Strategy. It is hidden until such a time when it is needed. Your parents are just behind the door. They are waiting for you with Champion, the Leader of the Princess Warriors. She is the greatest warrior of all." As they stood directly in front of the door, Clarity's teacher turned to leave. Alone in the hallway, Clarity was trembling as she reached to grab the doorknob and open the door. It swung slowly open. Before her stood a magnificent woman dressed in armor, with flowing red hair that danced around her. Her presence was overwhelming as the power contained within her filled the room and entered the hallway. She waved her hand for Clarity to enter.

As she did so, she saw a man and a woman standing behind the warrior. Clarity stopped cold. As her eyes took in the sight, she was filled with a knowing that before her stood her parents. They extended their arms to her, and she rushed into them. Finally, she was home. As they embraced, Champion made her way towards them. Her steps caused the entire room to rumble. She spoke as she neared. "Clarity, your parent's sacrifice of love to give you up in an effort to save you from the curse upon your family was seen by the Ruler of the Kingdom that Reigns Forever. In His infinite goodness and grace, He rescued them and you. You will be able to live united now and forever. They will be scribes for the Kingdom as well. We will all work together to win the final battle. It is coming soon, Clarity, and your written and spoken words will be needed more than ever before and upon which, the children you left behind at the Work House will be set free."

As Champion spoke, the final stone was added to Clarity's gilded gown. Her training, maturity, and healing were now complete. It had come to pass as Clarity had foreseen and would remain so within the Kingdom that Reigns Forever until the end of these present times.

The End

Book 5:
I Am Champion

I Am Champion

She was born in the Darklands. Her cries were quieted in order to spare her life. If the Wicked Ones of a rival pack found out that a new life had come into the world, they would have tried desperately to kidnap her, or worse, destroy her entirely. There was no value placed on individuals but only on becoming part of the pack. Learned, copied behaviors and styles of dress held significance as a way of determining which pack you belonged to. Lines were drawn across the villages of the Darklands to ensure that no one ventured from their designated area.

Only on the days of challenges when the warriors would enlist in fights to the death between rival packs would those lines be crossed. Violence was instilled into all of the children born into the Darklands. If they were weak, they would not be spared. Taken from their parents at a very early age, they were taught to fight one another as a way to determine who had superior skills and strength. If injuries were sustained during these fights, even by the victor, the injured child would be laughed at and taunted.

Into this world, Champion was born. Her parents were part of the Red Pack. The Red Pack was the strongest of all of the packs of the Darklands and held the most members. It was seen from early on that Champion had a strong, limber body and instinctive abilities in fighting. She seemed to almost be able to read the mind of her opponents and counter their moves with ease. Her training began early. Her father would slap her and then tell her not to cry. If she cried, he would slap her again. Her mother remained silent, knowing that any word of kindness from her would only cause her father to escalate his cruelty.

The only safe place Champion knew was in the loving arms of her grandmother, Caren. Caren hadn't been born in the Darklands. She was kidnapped from the other side of the mountains during a night raid executed by the Red Pack. She was brought to the Darklands as a very young woman and forced into labor within the leader's home. Soon, it became apparent that she held great beauty and wisdom. Her hair was curly and red. It seemed to dance with her every move. Her intelligence led her to question many of the rules in the leader's house, and he came to find that more often than not, her inquiries proved to save time or provide some other significant improvement. When the Red Pack leader saw this, he moved her into his main court and began to rely on her when making important decisions.

Soon, she met and fell in love with one of the court guards, Render. He, too, had been kidnapped and brought to the Darklands. He was held as a slave for the Red Pack and forced to do their bidding. He was much kinder than anyone else Caren had met in the Darklands. On days when she was not needed by the Red Pack leader, she would spend time in the courtyard reading or watching the birds. She often imagined that she could fly away as they did.

Render was sometimes assigned to watch the outer gate of the garden, and the two would share a quiet conversation. Render had been nearly grown when he was brought to the Darklands. Upon his initial arrival, he tried desperately to escape, only to be caught and thrown into a cell and left without food for many days. He finally decided that he would try to make a life for himself in this bad place rather than have his life placed in jeopardy each time he attempted to return home. His family had been killed during the raid, so there was little left for him to return home to anyway.

Render, as well as Caren, had both been told by their parents of the goodness of the Ruler of the Kingdom that Reigns Forever. They had walked in love and could still feel it beating within their hearts. This was what had drawn them together in the beginning. Once the leader of the Red Pack found out that Caren and Render cared deeply for one another, and after having grown fond of Caren for her goodness and for her help in running his pack, he released her from service to marry Render on the condition that she return twice a week to assist him. Caren quickly agreed. She and Render were married in the courtyard where they had met and began their life together.

Surely, the favor she had found with the Red Pack leader was a gift from the Ruler of the Kingdom that Reigns Forever. Their only child, Carina, was born two years later. She had been a sweet loving child but was removed from their care at six years old and raised in the warrior training ground. She was a skilled fighter, and due to her fast learning and having completed her training early, was placed in the Red Pack's strategy unit.

This is where future raids or invasions were planned. Carina believed in the Ruler of the Kingdom that Reigned Forever and often shared her belief with others that she came in contact with. While doing so, she met a Red Pack warrior named Ronkon. He was one of the top warriors in the Red Pack. His face and body were covered in scars received in battle. At first, he was captivated by Carina and her stories of the Ruler of the Kingdom that Reigns Forever, but when asked if he would like to change his heart and his life, he scoffed and said that "only a weak fool or a coward would give up being a warrior to become part of the Kingdom that Reigns Forever." Carina found Ronkon to be a cruel, vulgar man. She was forced to marry him by the Red Pack leader, who, having seen the two of them together, believed that any child from such a marriage would be an exceptional warrior and leader and so decreed that Carina and Ronkon would remain together for the rest of their lives and have children who would be trained to fight.

Upon the arrival of their first child, Carina vowed to never again bear children, for her heart was broken as she looked upon her daughter's face, realizing the horrible fate that lay before her. Born with her grandmother's beautiful red hair, she stood out from the beginning. Even so, Ronkon raged at Carina for baring a female child. Feeling that it suited this remarkable child, Carina name her Champion.

This seemed to ease Ronkon's anger. He found false pride in thinking that perhaps this child would be a champion after all. Carina remained silent, fearing that any wrong word from her would cause his wrath to fall upon her or on Champion in the form of slaps and shoves or violent shakings. Her silence became her strength, and her only goal was to protect her child. She must survive to ensure that Champion survived, and so

Carina remained silent for the rest of her years, speaking only to Champion in soft whispers, telling her of the Kingdom that Reigns Forever and of the love found there.

Ronkon would not allow Carina to cuddle or caress their child, telling her that it would make her weak and unable to fight. And so it was that Caren, Champion's grandmother, was the only one who ever showed Champion any affection. It was her mother, Carina, that would take her to visit her grandmother, and from these encounters, Champion found the love and kindness that would make her the exceptional warrior that she would one day be. Judgment must always be softened by mercy. This, along with other stories of the Kingdom that Reigns Forever, would set Champion on a path that would change the Darklands and the rest of the world forever.

A Champion Emerges

From Champion's beginning days in training, it was evident that the leader of the Red Pack had been correct in his assumption that the combination of Carina and Ronkon would bring forth an exceptional child. What he had not taken into account is that the wisdom passed down from her grandmother, Caren, to Champion would be his undoing. Many of the Red Pack's followers had come to believe in the Kingdom that Reigns Forever and had grown weary of the constant raids and wars that they were forced to take part in.

This was the plan all along. The Ruler of the Kingdom that Reigns Forever had sent Caren to the Darklands, knowing that her strong belief would heal those living in despair and set many of them free. He had protected her by sending her to live with the Red Pack leader in his home. No harm could come to her while there. Upon

Champion reaching her twentieth year, her cruel father was killed in a night raid. His body had been left behind, as the people of the Darklands had no respect for individual life. There would be no burial or even a small acknowledgment that he had ever lived.

Champion, her mother, and grandmother felt no sadness at this. Ronkon had been a cruel man, and his absence only improved their lives. Render allowed the now widowed Carina to move in with him and Caren. Champion came too. And this was the start of a movement that would set the people of the Darklands free. The dark, silent streets lacking any signs of life would one day be filled with dancing.

Until then, the Ruler of the Kingdom that Reigns Forever held his outstretched hand over them, preparing the way for freedom. Quietly at first, and then with growing boldness, Champion began to invite people to her home and there, with her mother and grandmother, would share the goodness of the Kingdom that Reigns Forever and of the great love of the Ruler.

Many hearts were changed. Little by little, the climate of the Darklands began to change, too. There were still those who believed that fighting and cruelty were the only ways to show power and strength, but daily, the number of those who began to believe in the love of the Kingdom that Reigns Forever grew. Some heard the voice that comes on the Warming Wind and would speak to others of what it foretold. The tiny, desolate house that was shared by Champion and her family was no longer adequate in size to hold meetings, and a new location needed to be secured.

Champion set about finding a new place to speak to the people about the Kingdom that Reigns Forever. In doing so, she approached a strange little man from the Blue Pack. He promised her he would be silent about her quest, but, unknown to Champion, this strange little man was selling information to the highest bidder regarding any news he heard on the street.

As it went, the highest bidder on this particular day was the leader of the Red Pack. Years later, Champion learned that the reason the man was so strange and little was the result of a curse that had been placed upon him of his own doing. He had once been a mighty warrior, stronger and larger than all the rest. He had grown weary of battle but was unwilling to accept the outcome of giving up the adulation he received from emerging victorious. Money and gifts were given to him by admirers, and he had amassed a great fortune.

Instead of living off of what he had already gained, he chose to sell information. This way, he could continue to grow his fortune without having to fight. Once he began this lifestyle, he grew more and more greedy. Enough was never enough. Even when those around him began to notice and comment on how he was dwindling in size, still, he would not stop.

The rumors spread quickly that his lack of fighting was causing his strength to wane. The longer he was away from battle, the more information he sold, the larger his fortune grew, the smaller he became until he stood before Champion, unrecognizable to the fighter he had once been.

Even his voice, which had been loud and booming, was now soft and shrill. His eyes, which had once been wide and able to see clearly the slightest movement from his foe, were now squinting and faded. His corruption had destroyed him more surely than any opponent he had ever faced. It was this strange little man that sold Champion out to the leader of the Red Pack and betrayed her. He told of the growing number of people who now believed in the Kingdom that Reigns Forever. He shared information about the new meeting place, the ruins of the original training arena up above the Darklands streets.

Upon the first meeting at this new site, the Red Pack leader was set to meet the Believers who gathered there and destroy them all. The plans were being made when the strange little man interrupted and said, "Destroy the head, and you destroy all." The Red Pack leader was enraged by this interruption and screamed, "Don't speak unless I request it!" He pulled his sword from its sheath and raised it over his head. He then finished with a hiss, "I'll slay you where you stand this very day." At just that moment, one of the leader's top warriors stepped in and said, "He may have a point, sir. Instead of destroying your people, destroy the one they follow. Then place the people into a training program to remove this new teaching from their minds. That may be the surest form of victory. Challenge their leader to a fight. You will be victorious. You will win." Allowing Self-Importance to be his guide, he agreed.

On the afternoon of the first meeting of the people who believed in the Kingdom that Reigns Forever, the Red Pack leader and some of his men showed up. They rode in on horseback, heavily armed. There were forty of them in all. The leader brought only enough men to contain the crowd, so convinced was he that his strategy would prove successful. As they entered the ruins of the training arena, the people rushed out of the way to avoid being trampled by the horses as they were unarmed and unprepared to fight. The dust rose high, and many were choking and coughing.

Champion stood on the platform overlooking the arena, for this is where she had planned to speak. The Red Pack leader rode directly to her as his followers cut off access to her by anyone that could have come to her aid. Shouting with a growl, he said, "You have no right to meet in this place. You will all leave immediately. This land belongs to me." Knowing this land was no longer assigned to any one pack, Champion replied, "This is no man's land. We are free to gather here as we wish." Knowing this would be her response, the Red Pack leader smiled and said, "Perhaps you and I should battle to see who will take control of it? Or would you prefer that we trample and kill your people instead? I can kill you, or I can kill them *all*. You decide." Champion would never have agreed to allow her people to be killed, and so she agreed to a one-on-one battle with the Red Pack leader. Neither she nor he understood at that moment the importance of the agreement they had just reached. The men on horseback created a ring around the arena where the battle was to take place. Champion jumped down from the platform onto the arena floor.

As she landed, the ground shook. The shaking reverberated throughout the land, and all who heard the stories called it "The Quake of the Champion." It is written into their books of history even as we speak today. Out of the crowd, Champion's grandmother came. She moved to within a hearing distance of Champion and spoke, "I have heard from the Warming Wind. You have been born for such a time as this." She moved away quickly as she felt the sword of the enemy coming at her. She was still a wise and knowing woman, kind and good and always aware.

As Champion absorbed the words she had just received from her grandmother, the Warming Wind blew over her, lifting her long, red hair. As the wind blew, her hair grew. It became wild and curled around her. Everyone stood in amazement at the sight of it. Champion could feel her strength growing too and knew that the Ruler of the Kingdom that Reigns Forever was with her and would ensure that she would win this battle, and through it, her people would be freed.

From upon horseback, the Red Pack leader charged her. He swung his sword towards her. As he neared, her hair unwound, and all could see that she was now fitted with beautiful gilded armor. She wore the Helmet of Salvation, the Breastplate of Righteousness, and the Belt of Truth. In one hand was the Sword of the Word, and in the other was the Shield of Faith, and upon her feet, she wore the shoes of the Gospel of Peace. Against such armor, there is no defense! The Red Pack leader slid down from his horse and fell to the ground. He shook with fear at the powerful image of Champion standing before him. Her sword held high, her hair swirling about her like flame, her armor glistening in the sun and her eyes reflecting the truth of the love of the Kingdom that Reigns Forever were too much for him to bear. He fell before her and begged for mercy.

With a quick movement, she stood over him and spoke, "You and all who follow your evil ways are forever removed from this land. It will no longer be known as the Darklands with streets of mourning and death. The battle cry will now be one of the victory of life! By this decree from the Ruler of the Kingdom that Reigns forever, this place will be known as the Land of Quiet Streams." As she spoke, the platform she had once stood upon broke in two! Clear, vibrant water sprang forth from it and ran down the hillside and into the streets below.

At once, the land became green with grass and shrubs and trees. People came from their homes and viewed this transformation in amazement. The remaining warriors on horseback slid down from their saddles and fell to the ground and began to worship Champion. She spoke in a clear but gentle voice and said, "I am not the Ruler, nor should I be worshipped. I am simply a champion for the cause of the Ruler of the Kingdom that Reigns Forever. Follow him. Worship him, and your days shall be fulfilled."

As she spoke, a gentle breeze came upon the crowd. It spoke with the voice of the Warming Wind and said, "I am with you always. Even to the ends of this world." So moved was the crowd by this feeling of love that no one spoke. It was Champion who finally said, "I must leave now. For as much as it was unnecessary for me to fight today, there will come a day when I must fight a final battle for the freedom of people everywhere. The plans are in motion, and as we speak, an army is rising up. Leaders are being called and trained. Some to fight, some to heal, some to worship, and some to write.

You will be called upon, too. Ready yourselves. Watch and wait. When the time has come, you will know by the signs." She turned to see her mother and grandmother holding one another as tears ran down their faces. Some were of sadness to see Champion go, and some were of pride and joy at seeing her become who she was always meant to be. Champion approached them. Her movements were more graceful now, and with every step, the earth shook. Her grandmother spoke first. She reached up and gently touched Champion's face and said, "I have always known that you were a great warrior, but such as this, Champion, I have never seen. The Ruler of the Kingdom that Reigns Forever has used my kidnapping, my daughter's forced marriage, and all of these wicked plans to raise up a leader. He has taken what was meant for harm and will use it for good. You are his instrument, Champion. I may not see you again in this life, for my time here has nearly come to an end, but I will see you one day on the other side, where my spirit will live forever." She kissed Champion on the cheek and, with tears still flowing, walked silently away.

Champion's mother, beaming with pride, came next. It was Champion that spoke first this time. "Mother, you must help these people learn about the Ruler of the Kingdom that Reigns Forever. You must remain with them until the final battle and help them prepare." Her mother smiled her knowing smile and replied, "Yes, and you must go." They stood in silence, looking at each other as if trying to memorize every line of the other's face, knowing that their reunion would not happen for quite some time. After many moments passed, they embraced. They held tight and then abruptly moved away. Champion turned on her heel, for she did not want her mother to see the tears streaming down her face. "Be strong, my Champion." Her mother cried out as Champion strode away. "Know that I have always loved you. Know that I will always love you." Without looking back, Champion made her way up the hill.

The sun was beginning to set, and as she walked, she became nothing more than a mist. She was on her way to another hillside, to a shimming orb. There she would meet her Princess Warriors. The Protectors, the Worshipers, the Healers, and the Scribes. She would lead them to victory in a final battle. This was her destiny. This was the fabric of her life, woven together by those who had come before her. She had become a warrior prepared for a battle to set all people free.

She would fulfill the legacy of her namesake. From this day forward, she would be known as a powerful handmaiden in the Kingdom that Reigns Forever. A true Champion.

The End

Epilogue

And it came to pass that after their training, Marvelous, Glorious, Victorious, Clarity and Champion joined together as allies. The voice that comes as a Warming Wind carried them through many battles, and the Kingdom that Reigns Forever came upon the entirety of every village and outpost to bring love, peace, freedom, and truth to all.

CPSIA information can be obtained
at www.ICGtesting.com
Printed in the USA
LVHW050312161221
706369LV00010B/738

9 781637 695500